Haunted House Activity Book

Jessica Mazurkiewicz

DOVER PUBLICATIONS, INC.
Mineola, New York

Copyright

Copyright © 2010 by Dover Publications, Inc.
All rights reserved.

Bibliographical Note

Haunted House Activity Book is a new work, first published by Dover
Publications, Inc. in 2010.

International Standard Book Number
ISBN-13: 978-0-486-47522-6
ISBN-10: 0-486-47522-0

Manufactured in the United States by Courier Corporation
47522001
www.doverpublications.com

Note

Get ready for an eerie Halloween adventure as you travel through this haunted house, and solve puzzles, codes, and brainteasers along the way! Forty-three activities include hidden pictures, crossword puzzles, spot-the-differences, follow-the-dots, number codes, mazes, and more—each page featuring spooky characters such as ghosts, bats, spiders, and other Halloween favorites. Do your best to solve each puzzle, but if you get stuck, there is a Solutions section that begins on page 52. Are you brave enough to enter this haunted house?

Count how many ghosts are in the picture of the
haunted house, then write the number
in the space on the tombstone.

__ __ __ __ __ __ __

Unscramble the letters on the bats to find the name of
some creatures that live in the haunted house.
Write its name on the blanks provided.

Fill in the missing letters in each word to spell out the names of three animals that often lurk about the haunted house.

Guide the ghost through the graveyard
to the haunted house.

Look carefully at this picture of a spooky attic.

Now circle five things in this picture of the
spooky attic that make it different from
the one on the previous page.

Ghoul
Spirit
Ghost

Specter
Phantom
Poltergeist

The names of six supernatural beings are listed above.
Look down and across to find them
in the word search.

Circle the ghost that haunts the house at the bottom of the page. Only one can fit!

Connect the dots from 1 to 37 to see
who built this web.

Find and circle the letters H, A, U, N, T, E, and D hidden in the picture of the haunted house.

Count how many bats are in the picture above, then write the number in the space on the haunted house.

Follow the paths from each creature to find out which one will reach the haunted house.

The number next to each picture tells you where its name belongs in the crossword puzzle on the opposite page.

Using the pictures as your guide,
fill in the missing letters.

start

start

end

Only one of these two cats can make it to the end
by following the path. Solve the maze to find
out which one.

18

Look carefully at all the creatures sitting outside
the haunted house, then circle the ones
that belong inside it.

19

There is a wall of creepy old portraits inside this
haunted house! Look at the portraits carefully,
and circle the two that are exactly the same.

Find and circle the letters S, P, O, O, K, and Y hidden
in the picture of the haunted stairwell.

Look carefully at this picture of a haunted house
and graveyard on a hill.

Now circle six things in this picture of the haunted house and graveyard on a hill that make it different from the one on the previous page.

There are three sets of identical bats flying around this room in the haunted house. Draw a line connecting each pair of matching bats.

Look carefully at the four haunted houses in the picture above. Find and circle the one that is different from the rest.

This little vampire bat needs your help! Find and circle the six pieces of garlic that were hidden to try and scare her away.

The rat has a message for you! Use the number code to arrange the words on the correct blanks, and find out what it is.

Help the skull by finding and circling the five bones hidden around the haunted house.

Use the number code to fill in the blanks and find out what the raven has to say.

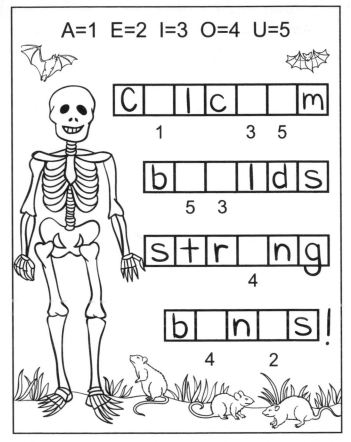

A=1 E=2 I=3 O=4 U=5

C		l	c		m
	1			3	5

b			l	d	s
	5	3			

s	t	r		n	g
			4		

b		n		s	!
	4		2		

Fill in the blanks by using the number code, and find
out what the skeleton wants to tell you.

There are three ravens hiding in the picture above.
Find and circle all three.

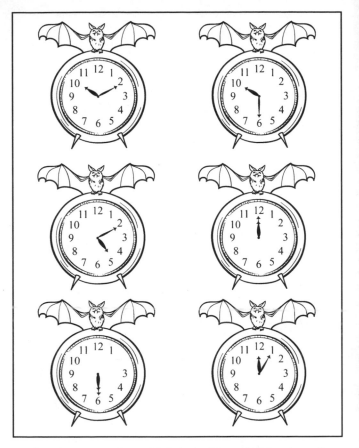

Another name for midnight is "the witching hour."
Can you find and circle the clock whose hands
point to 12 o'clock?

One of these spiders has six legs instead of eight!
Find and circle the spider with only six legs.

HAUNTED

moo☐

☐o☐se

☐re☐

c☐t

spi**d**er

Using each letter from the word HAUNTED one time,
complete each word next to a picture above.
One blank has been filled in for you.

raven

bat

cat

rat

spider

```
        A
      B   T
    L C A I
    R A T N
  S P I D B L
E A C O C A T U
J R A N N T J T
S L E R A V S T
T A R S P I D E R
S O C A L E S C I
R A V E N L A E D
M A A C T A R T B
```

Some animals that live inside the haunted house are
shown in the picture above. Find and circle their names
in the word search. Look down and across.

Look carefully at the tombstones in the picture above.
Find and circle the two that are identical.

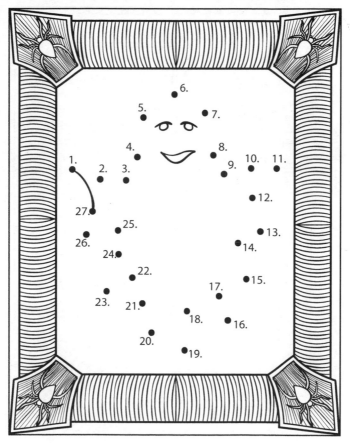

Connect the dots from 1 to 27 to see who is
lurking in the picture frame.

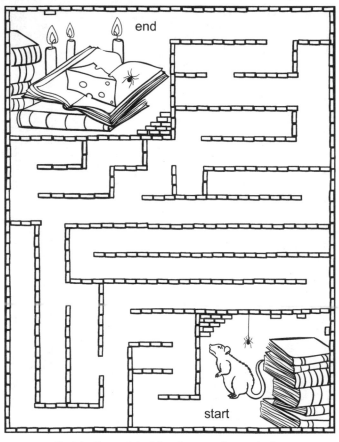

Guide the rat to his cheese through the
spooky library maze.

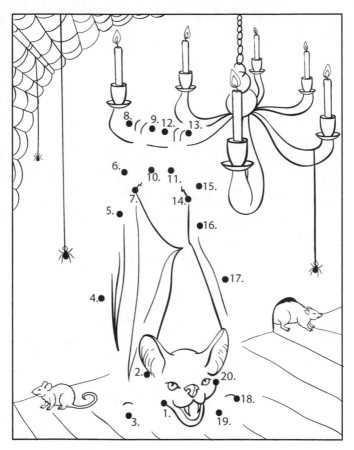

Connect the dots from 1 to 20 to see who is hanging from the chandelier.

There are three ghosts hiding in the picture of the graveyard. Find and circle all three.

HAUNTED

hat

Using only the letters in the word HAUNTED,
spell out as many words as you can.
One word has been filled in for you.

Find and circle the spider that is exactly the same as
the one in the web in the top left corner.

Unscramble the letters on the tombstones to find out
what lurks about the haunted house.
Write its name on the blank spaces provided.

Creepy ✳ Eerie ✳ Dreadful

Fearsome ✳ Ghoulish

Ghastly ✳ Spooky ✳ Strange

Unearthly ✳ Weird

All the words listed above describe the haunted house.
Search for them in the word search on the
opposite page.

```
U N N T E M L L Y W P
S G F E A R S O M E E
P I H B J S X I N I S
O B U O E T I N S R T
O G T N U I L T C D R
K V A D E L R E L Y A
Y T D E S A I L Z E N
C N T R M G R S H O G
U W I F E H L T H S E
L P E L N A L G H A I
A X E Y A S D E A L N
R A R Z R T S F U H Y
F L I E C L W T U B R
C R E E P Y A O O L Y
Y C T T V R A E G M N
```

Search down, across, and diagonally to find the words
from the list on the previous page.

45

Look carefully at this picture of the haunted house.

Now circle six things in this picture of the haunted house that make it different from the one on the previous page.

Connect the dots from 1 to 16 to see who is perched
in the tree outside the haunted house.

Draw a line from each spooky creature to its home.

Count how many spiders are in the picture of the giant web, then write the number in the space on the tree.

Find and circle the letters G, H, O, S, and T hidden in the picture of the haunted ballroom.

page 4

page 5

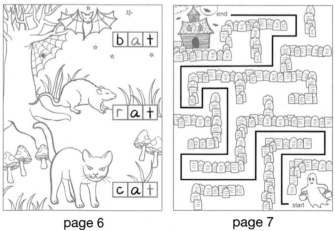

page 6

page 7

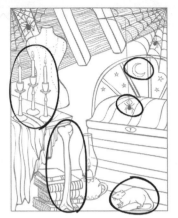

page 9

page 10

page 11

page 12

page 13

page 14

page 15

page 17

page 18

page 19

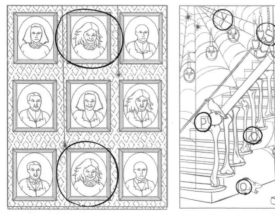

page 20

page 21

page 23

page 24

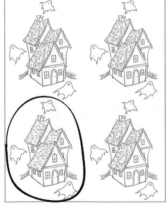

page 25

page 26

page 27

page 28

page 29

page 30

page 31

page 32

page 33

page 34

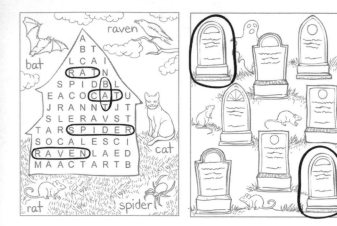

page 35

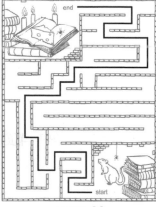

page 36

page 37

page 38

page 39

page 40

HAUNTED	
hat	than
had	then
hen	thud
head	the
heat	tuna
hunt	due
ant	duet
aunt	dent
neat	dune

(possible answers)
page 41

page 42

page 43

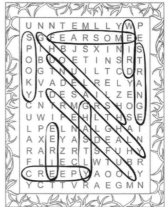

page 45

page 47

page 48

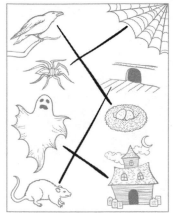

page 49

page 50

page 51

63